PEARSON
LANGUAGE
CENTRAL

ELD Newcomer

Grades 3–5

Glenview, Illinois • Boston, Massachusetts • Chandler, Arizona •
Upper Saddle River, New Jersey

Illustrations   George Ulrich and Diane Paterson

Photographs
Every effort has been made to secure permission and provide appropriate credit for photographic material.
The publisher deeply regrets any omission and pledges to correct errors called to its attention in subsequent editions.

Unless otherwise acknowledged, all photographs are the property of Pearson Education, Inc.

Photo locators denoted as follows: Top (T), Center (C), Bottom (B), Left (L), Right (R), Background (Bkgd)

4 (C) Getty Images, (C) Swerve/Alamy Images; **5** (B) David R. Frazier Photolibrary Inc/Alamy Images; **6** (C) photos_alyson/Taxi/Getty Images, (CL) Davis Barber/PhotoEdi, (BL) ©Blend Images/Alamy, (CR) Getty Images; **7** (C) ©Jupiterimages/Comstock Premium/Alamy, (CL) ©Blend Images/Alamy, (CR) ©Eric Fowke/PhotoEdit, (C) Swerve/Alamy Images; **8** (C) Ian Shaw/Alamy Images, (C) ©Jupiterimages/Comstock Premium/Alamy, (CR) ©Adriane Moll/zefa/Corbis, (C) Corbis/Jupiter Images, (C) ©Corbis Super RF/Alamy; **9** (C) Michael Newman/ PhotoEdit; **10** (CL) Michael Newman/PhotoEdit, (C) ©Blend Images/Alamy, (CR) Getty Images. **11** (C) ©Corbis Premium RF/Alamy.

ISBN-13: 978-0-328-38450-1
ISBN-10:   0-328-38450-X

15   17
CC1

Table of Contents

Welcome to School!

school

Today is your first day at school.

bus

You can come by **bus**.

crosswalk

You can walk to school.
Cross the street at the **crosswalk**.

door

Come in through
the door.

First, go to the office
for information.

locker

Put your things
in your locker.

Then, go to your classroom.

You can go
up the stairs.

You can go
down the stairs.

stairs

You can use
a **ramp**.

ramp

You can walk
down the **hall**.

You can read a book in the **library**.

You can play games in the **gym**.

You can make music in the **music room**.

You can draw a picture in the **art room**.

It's recess! Go to the **playground**.

Get a drink from
the **water fountain**.

If you get hurt, go
to the **nurse's office**.

It's time for lunch.
You can eat in the lunch room.

Ask your teacher to
go to the rest room.

It's assembly day.
Go to the auditorium.

Do you like to use the
computer room?

It's time to go home.
Look for the **EXIT sign**.
We'll see you tomorrow!

1 My Class

Tell what you know.

Good-bye, Ana.

Hi. My name is Alan.

Hi. I'm Lara. This is Josie.

Say the words.

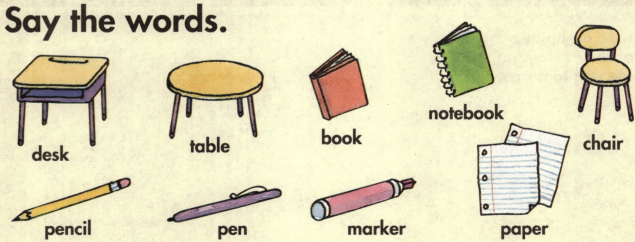

desk

table

book

notebook

chair

pencil

pen

marker

paper

Say the numbers. Read the words.

	0	zero
	1	one
	2	two
	3	three
	4	four
	5	five
	6	six
	7	seven
	8	eight
	9	nine
	10	ten

How many? Count the items.

I have two notebooks.

I have one notebook.

Items	desk 1	+	desk 2	=	how many?
1. notebooks	2	+	1	+	3
2. pencils		+		=	
3. books		+		=	
4. markers		+		=	

Count. Write the number.

1.  + = _____

2.  + = _____

3. + = _____

Circle the picture.

1. desk		2. pencil			
3. table		4. notebook			
5. marker		6. book			

Write the number.

I have one book. What do you have?

I have _____ books.

I have _____ pencils.

I have _____ notebooks.

Tell what you know.

Look at the pictures. Say the words.

letter
address
street
house
city
state
zip code
area code
phone number
phone

Say the alphabet.

Aa Bb Cc Dd Ee Ff Gg Hh Ii
Jj Kk Ll Mm Nn Oo Pp Qq Rr
Ss Tt Uu Vv Ww Xx Yy Zz

Write your name. Spell it.

My name is Kenji. K-e-n-j-i.

My name is _____.

Write your phone number.
Ask a partner.

My phone number is (312) 555-7307. What's your phone number?

My phone number is

(_____) _____.

My friend's phone number is

(_____) _____.

Send a letter to a friend.
Write the address.

17 Maple Street, Miami, Florida 33143

What's your address?

Luis Mendoza
17 Maple Street
Miami, Florida
33143

Read the rhyme with a partner.

Say the letters A, B, C.

Point to D, E, F, and G.

Write an X on H, I, J.

Say and write the letter K. _____

Circle L, M, N, O, P.

Color Q, R, S, and T.

Write the letters U and V. _____ _____

Draw a line through W, X, Y, Z.

Make a phone book. page 71

Ask.

Write.

Cut.

Staple.

Circle the word.

1.		house phone	2.  crayon pen
3.		phone number phone	4. book chair

Write the letters.

a b ___ d e f ___ h i j ___ l m ___
___ p q ___ s ___ u v w ___ y z

Write your phone number.

I can. ✓

☐ I can say my name and address.

☐ I can say my area code and phone number.

☐ I can say the alphabet.

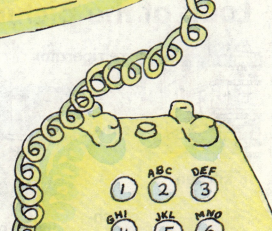

Tell what you know.

I live in this house. Where do you live?

I live in this apartment building. I live on the second floor

Look at the pictures. Say the words.

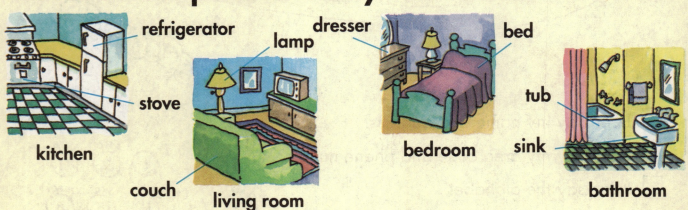

refrigerator

lamp

dresser

bed

stove

tub

kitchen

bedroom

sink

couch

living room

bathroom

Say more words.

door

bed

chair

table

Match each thing with a room.

bedroom

bathroom

kitchen

living room

couch

tub

stove

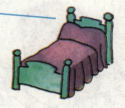
bed

Ask a partner.

Room	What do you do there?
1. bathroom	*I wash my hands.*
2. kitchen	
3. living room	

Write the name of the room.

1. _bedroom_

2. _____

 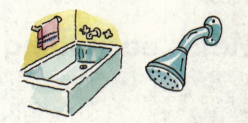

3. _____

4. _____

Tell about a room. page 73

Cut.   Draw.

Write.

Write. Use a word in the box.

1. _____

2. _____

3. _____

4. _____

Circle the room.

1.

kitchen
living room
bathroom

2.

bedroom
bathroom
kitchen

I can.

☐ I can name the rooms in a home.

☐ I can name and write about things in a home.

☐ I can talk to friends about my home and their homes.

4 My Family

Look at the pictures. Say the words.

sister   aunt   uncle   brother

mother

grandmother

grandfather

father

Read the story.

"My name is Rosa. This is my family."

1. brother dad mom cousin sister

2. My **mom** writes stories.

3. My **dad** is a teacher.

4. My **sister**, my **brother**, my **cousin**, and I play soccer.

How do you feel? Say the words.

happy

sad

feelings

angry

scared

How do you feel today?

Write and draw.

I feel _____.

Circle the words.

children   mom and dad

children   mom and dad

grandmother   grandfather

cousin   aunt

Act out the words. Practice with a partner.

How do you feel?

I feel scared.

happy

angry

scared

sad

Play a game. Match the cards. page 75

Write the words. Use the words in the box.

_____ _____ _____ _____

This is my family.

| mother |
| father |
| grandfather |
| aunt |
| uncle |
| brother |
| sister |
| grandmother |

_____ _____ _____ _____

Show the feeling. Draw.

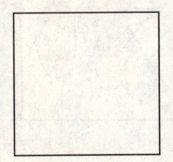 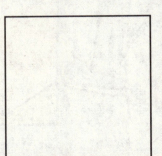  

happy   **sad**   **scared**   **angry**

I can.

☐ I can name people in a family.

☐ I can say the names of feelings.

☐ I can act out feelings.

Tell what you know.

Say the times.

It's twelve o'clock.

It's three o'clock.

It's six o'clock.

It's nine o'clock.

Say the numbers.

11	12	13	14	15	16
eleven	twelve	thirteen	fourteen	fifteen	sixteen

17	18	19	20	21
seventeen	eighteen	nineteen	twenty	twenty-one

Say the colors.

red   orange   yellow   green   blue   purple

Say the shapes.

circle   square   triangle   rectangle

Find the shapes in your classroom.

Work with a partner.

Item	Shape
1. *clock*	*circle*
2.	
3.	
4.	

Circle the word.

1.		orange yellow red	2.  green purple blue
3.		orange red blue	4.  green yellow blue

Color the shapes. Make a pattern.

pattern

1.

2.

3.

Write the numbers. Say the times.

1. _8:00_   2. _____   3. _____   4. _____   5. _____

Play bingo. page 77

Write the times.

1. _____ 2. _____ 3. _____ 4. _____ 5. _____

Circle the word.

1. red / blue / yellow

2. orange / blue / red

3. yellow / blue / orange

4. green / orange / yellow

Color the shapes. Make a pattern.

1.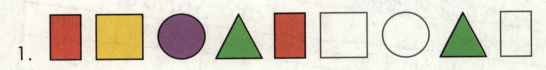

2.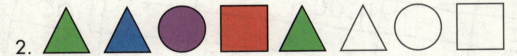

3.

I can.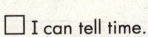

☐ I can tell time.

☐ I can say   .   ☐ I can say   .

☐ I can count to 21.

6 My Week

Tell what you know.

Say the days of the week.

Sunday	Monday	Tuesday	Wednesday	Thursday	Friday	Saturday
1	2	3	4	5	6	7

Say the months of the year.

Look at the pictures. Put them in order.

They have art on Wednesday.

They have music on Tuesday.

They have library on Friday.

Circle the word.

1. **Tuesday, Wednesday, _____ , Friday**

    Monday   Sunday   Thursday   Saturday

2. **Monday, _____ , Wednesday, Thursday**

    Sunday   Friday   Tuesday   Saturday

3. **January, _____ , March, April**

    July   May   February   December

4. **March, April, May, _____**

    January   February   June   August

When do you have class?

Work with a partner.

Class	Day	My Partner's Class	Day
1.		1.	
2.		2.	
3.		3.	

Make a class calendar. page 79

Cut.

Paste.

Write.

Draw.

What holidays do you know?

Write them on the class calendar. Work with a partner.

Circle the word.

1. **Sunday, _____ , Tuesday, Wednesday**
   Friday   Thursday   Saturday   Monday

2. **Tuesday, Wednesday, _____ , Friday**
   Monday   Friday   Thursday   Saturday

3. **May, June, _____ , August**
   August   December   January   July

4. **February, March, April, _____**
   August   June   May   February

Write about yourself.

I have art on _____ .

I have music on _____ .

My favorite subject is _____ .

I can. ✔

- ☐ I can say the days of the week.
- ☐ I can say the months of the year.
- ☐ I can say subject names.
- ☐ I can talk about my schedule.

7 My School

Tell what you know.

This is the classroom.

This is the nurse's office.

This is the girls' rest room.

This is the office.

This is the library.

This is my school.

What time is it? Say the times.

It's one thirty.

3:30

It's three thirty.

It's six thirty.

9:30

It's nine thirty.

Who's this? Say the names.

principal

teacher

librarian

student

secretary

Draw a line from the people to the places.

Name the people and places.

1.

2.

3.

a.

b.

c.

Draw the times.

1. It's two thirty.

2. It's eleven thirty.

3. It's nine thirty.

4. It's four thirty.

Do the puzzle.

Write the words you know first.

Across →

1.
2.

3.
4.

Down ↓

5. 
6.

7.

Down word: **secretary**

Write a story. ✂ page 81

Tell it to a partner.

My name is _____ .

I _____ .

My name is Ana. I go to school at 8:30.

Who are the people in your school? Write.

My English teacher's name is _____ .

My principal's name is _____ .

The librarian's name is _____ .

Draw the times.

1. It's three thirty.   2. It's one thirty.   3. It's five thirty.   4. It's four thirty.

Draw a line from the people to the places.

1.

a.

2.

b.

3.

c.

I can.

☐ I can tell time.

☐ I can name the people in my school.

Say the words.

pants

T-shirt

raincoat

backpack

shorts

shoes

umbrella

dress

jacket

sweater

Say the words.

 It's rainy.

 It's sunny.

 It's windy.

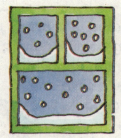 It's snowy.

 It's cloudy.

Draw a line from the weather to the clothes.

 It's snowy.

 It's rainy.

 It's sunny.

 scarf

 umbrella

 raincoat

 sandals

 shorts

 jacket

 hat

 T-shirt

Circle the word.

1.	pants shorts jacket	2. hat T-shirt sandals
3.	raincoat umbrella scarf	4. T-shirt shorts dress

Read the descriptions with a partner.

Hi! My name is Maria. I'm wearing a yellow shirt, brown pants, and white shoes. I have an orange jacket.

Hi! My name is Chris. I'm wearing a green sweater, blue pants, and black shoes. I have a green backpack.

Practice with a partner.

I'm wearing a green shirt, black pants, and brown shoes. I have a red jacket. What are you wearing?

I'm wearing a blue dress and black shoes. I have a red backpack.

Draw and write your own description.
Read it to a friend.

Hi! My name is _____.

I'm wearing _____,

_____, and _____.

I have a _____.

Play the matching game.  page 83

It's sunny. I'm wearing shorts.

It's rainy. I have an umbrella.

match

Draw the clothes.

1.

green jacket

2.

blue pants

3.

red T-shirt

Write the weather.

1. It's _____ .

2. It's _____ .

3. It's _____ .

I can.

☐ I can say the names of clothing.

☐ I can say the weather.

☐ I can talk about my clothes.

Tell what you know.

Say the words.

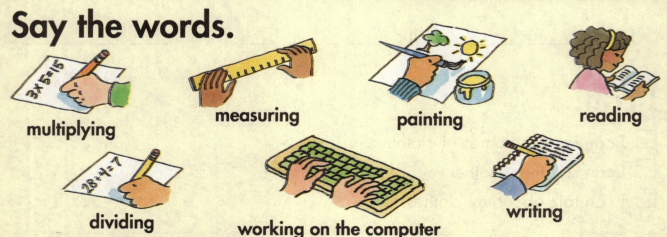

multiplying

measuring

painting

reading

dividing

working on the computer

writing

Say the words.

adding

subtracting

drawing

kicking the ball

singing

running

playing soccer

making a map

Draw the pictures. Say the words.

1.
I'm multiplying.

2.
I'm drawing.

3.
I'm playing soccer.

Practice with a partner.

What are you doing?

I'm writing a story.

Draw lines from the people to the items.

What do they need?

1.  I'm dividing.

2. I'm painting.

3. I'm measuring.

4. I'm playing soccer.

5. I'm reading.

a.

b.

c.

d.

e.

Act it out. Have a partner guess. page 85

Reading?

Reading

Read the story.

Circle the word.

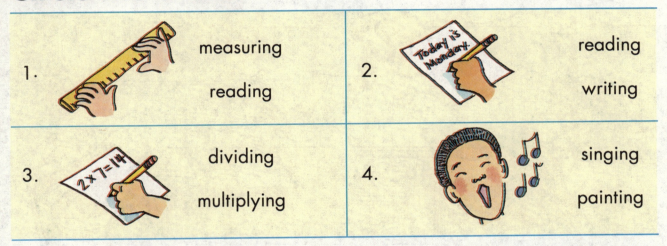

1. measuring / reading
2. reading / writing
3. dividing / multiplying
4. singing / painting

Write the words.

1. I'm _____.
2. I'm _____.
3. I'm _____.

I can. ✔

☐ I can read and write about what I do at school.
☐ I can talk about what I do at school.

Tell what you know.

Say the words.

apple   banana   juice   sandwich   grapes

milk   taco   pizza   cookie

Say the words.

corn

chicken

broccoli

rice

potato

bread

ice cream

hamburger

Draw pictures. Write the words.

What do you like to eat?

1.

I like to eat _____.

2.

I like to eat _____.

3.

I like to eat _____.

4.

I like to eat _____.

Ask your friends. Take a survey.

Name	Likes To Eat
1. *Tina*	*pizza*
2.	
3.	
4.	

What do you like to eat?

I like to eat pizza.

Read the Story.

For breakfast, I like to eat cereal, toast, and an orange. I like to drink juice.

For lunch, I like to eat a sandwich, an apple, and cookies. I like to drink milk.

For dinner, I like to eat chicken, rice, and salad. I like to drink milk.

Draw a picture. Write the words.

What do you like?

For _____,

I like to eat _____,

_____, and

_____.

I like to drink _____.

Make a meal. page 87

Cut.

Choose.

Glue.

Write.

Draw the food.

1.	2.	3.	4.
apple	sandwich	pizza	banana

Write the words.

1. _____ 2. _____ 3. _____ 4. _____

Write. Use the words in the box.

breakfast

lunch

dinner

1. _____ 2. _____ 3. _____

I can. ✔

☐ I can say the names of food.

☐ I can say what I like to eat.

☐ I can write about the foods I like.

☐ I can ask my friends what they like.

Tell what you know.

math

science

social studies

reading

Look at these pictures. Say the words.

plant

$$14 - 8 = 6$$
times · minus

$$7 \times 5 = 35$$
problems

story

globe

history book

rocks

Say more words.

Earth

map

country

OUR FAVORITE FOODS

bar graph

My name is Luz

sentence

capital letter   period

Circle the word.

1.

rocks
globe
history book

2.

story
map
period

3.

plant
globe
graph

4. **14 – 8 = 6**

map
problem
capital letter

Circle the picture.

1.

I study science.
I'm learning about plants.

2. My name is Luz .

I study reading.
I'm reading a sentence.

Circle the sentence.

1. **5 x 8 = 40**

   Five times eight equals forty.

   Five minus eight equals forty.

2. **14 – 2 = 12**

   Fourteen times two equals twelve.

   Fourteen minus two equals twelve.

Read the story.

I study science in school. I'm learning about **rocks**.

I'm learning about **Earth**.

I'm learning about **plants**.

Write about yourself.

1. I study _____ in school.

2. I'm learning about _____ .

Show a subject. ✂ page 89

Cut.　　　　　**Draw and color.**　　　　　**Paste.**

What subject? Circle the correct one.

1.

math   science
reading   social studies

2.

math   science
reading   social studies

3.

math   science
reading   social studies

4.

math   science
reading   social studies

Write. Use a word in the box.

1.

_____

2.

_____

3.

_____

story

globe

rocks

Draw.

1.

plant

2.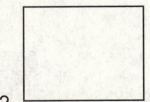

globe

I can.

☐ I can say the names of school subjects.

☐ I can say what I learn in school.

12 After School

Tell what you know.

Say the words.

read a book

play basketball

clean my room

listen to music

go to the library

ride my bike

Practice with a friend.

Ask your friends. Take a survey.

Name	Likes to
1. *Mike*	*listen to music*
2.	
3.	
4.	

Draw pictures. Write the words.

What do you like to do after school?

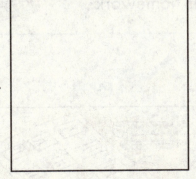

1.

First I _____

_____.

2.

Then I _____

_____.

3.

Then I _____

_____.

Read the sentences.

She's doing her homework.

He's playing soccer.

He's reading a book.

She's eating a snack.

Circle the sentences.

What are they doing?

1. He's riding a bike.

   He's playing soccer.

2.  She's reading a book.

   She's playing the piano.

3.  He's eating a snack.

   He's doing his homework.

4.  She's listening to music.

   She's talking to her friends.

Make a book. ✂ page 91

Write sentences.

Cut and staple the pages.

Read it to a friend.

Draw pictures.

What are they doing?

1. [ ]

He's reading a book.

2. [ ]

She's playing basketball.

3. [ ]

She's eating a snack.

4. [ ]

He's doing his homework.

Write the sentences.

1. *She's playing the piano.*

2. _____.

3. _____.

4. _____.

I can. ✔

- [ ] I can talk about what I do after school.
- [ ] I can write about what I do after school.
- [ ] I can ask my friends what they do after school.
- [ ] I can write about what my friends do after school.

Tell what you know.

Say the words.

library	post office	supermarket	bus stop
laundromat	park	mall	movie theater

Circle the word.

1.

park

post office

mall

2.

supermarket

bus stop

park

3.

laundromat

library

post office

Say the words.

checking out a book

mailing a letter

buying food

waiting for a bus

washing clothes

playing basketball

shopping at the mall

watching a movie

Practice with a friend.

What are you doing?

I'm mailing a letter.

Say the directions.

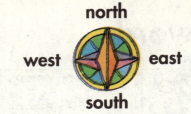

Look at the map. Write the directions.

Which way?

Which way to the school?

1. *Go north.*

Which way to the post office?

2. Go _____.

Which way to the library?

3. Go _____.

Which way to the police station?

4. Go _____.

Make a map. ✂ page 93

Cut out the places.

Glue places on the map.

Show it to a friend.

Write the directions.

____

____ ____

____

Circle the sentence.

What are they doing?

1. They're shopping.

   They're mailing a letter.

   They're washing clothes.

2. They're playing basketball.

   They're checking out books.

   They're buying food.

3. She's watching a movie.

   She's buying food.

   She's washing clothes.

4. He's waiting for a bus.

   He's mailing a letter.

   He's shopping.

I can.

☐ I can talk about places in my neighborhood.

☐ I can write about places in my neighborhood.

☐ I can say and write directions.

☐ I can make a map.

Tell what you know.

Look. Say.

dollar

penny

nickel

dime

quarter

change

Say the words.

one penny	=	1 cent
one nickel	=	5 cents
one dime	=	10 cents
one quarter	=	25 cents
one dollar	=	100 cents

How much does it cost? Circle.

I shop at the store. I buy a ball. It costs 25 cents.

one penny   one quarter   one nickel

I shop at the store. I buy a pencil. It costs 1 cent.

one penny   one quarter   one nickel

I shop at the store. I buy a banana. It costs 10 cents.

one penny   one dime   one nickel

I shop at the store. I buy a cookie. It costs 5 cents.

one penny   one dime   one nickel

Practice with a partner.

How much does it cost?

The crayon costs 5 cents.

Count. Write a number from the box.

 + = _____ cents

quarter   dime

40   130   35   110

 + dime = _____ cents

dollar   dime

 +  +  = _____ cents

dollar   quarter   nickel

How many cents? Take turns.

How many cents are in a nickel?

A nickel is five cents.

How many cents are in a quarter?

A quarter is twenty-five cents.

Go to the store. Act it out. ✂ page 95

May I please have a banana?

A banana costs 12 cents.

Here is one dime and two pennies.

Thank you.

Cut.   **Say.**   **Match.**

Circle.

1. 　penny　nickel
　　　　　　　dime　quarter

2. 　penny　nickel
　　dime　quarter

3. 　penny　nickel
　　dime　quarter

4. 　penny　nickel
　　dime　quarter

Match.

10 cents　　　　　penny

5 cents　　　　　quarter

25 cents　　　　　dollar

1 cent　　　　　　dime

100 cents　　　　nickel

I can.

☐ I can say: **penny**, **nickel**, **dime**, **quarter**, **dollar**, **change**.
☐ I can talk about buying things.
☐ I can count cents.

Activity Pages

Cut. Fasten. Spin.

Cut out the pages to the phone book.

Name _____

Phone Number _____

Name _____

Phone Number _____

Name _____

Phone Number _____

Name _____

Phone Number _____

Name _____

Phone Number _____

Name _____

Phone Number _____

Name _____

Phone Number _____

Name _____

Phone Number _____

Draw a home.

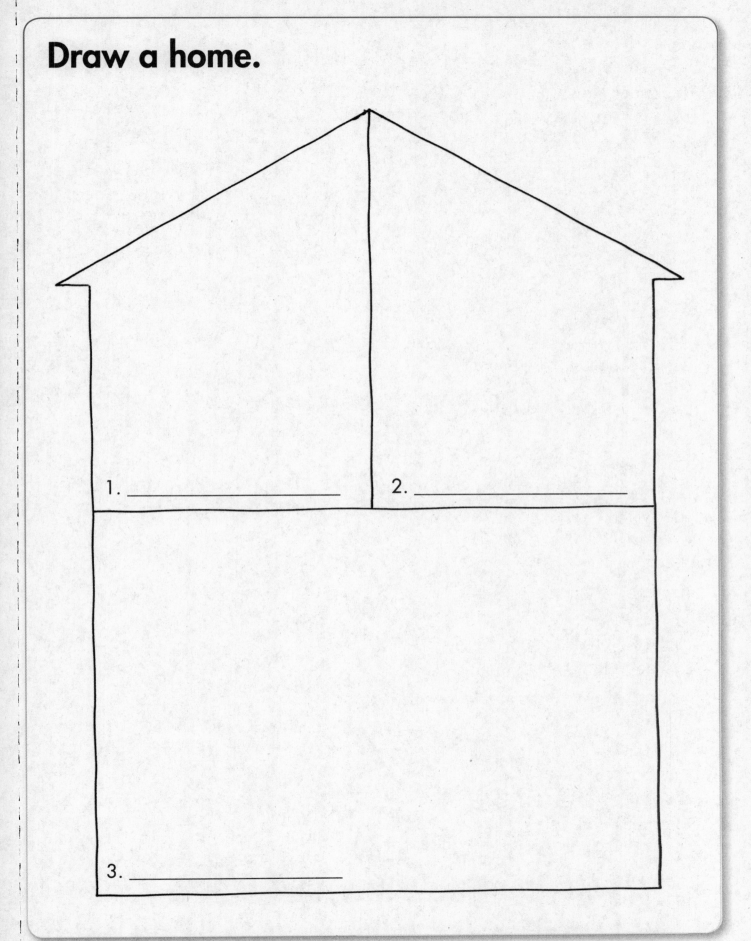

1. _____

2. _____

3. _____

Cut out the cards. Play a game.

happy

sad

angry

scared

Cut out the clocks. Play bingo.

Cut out the calendar.

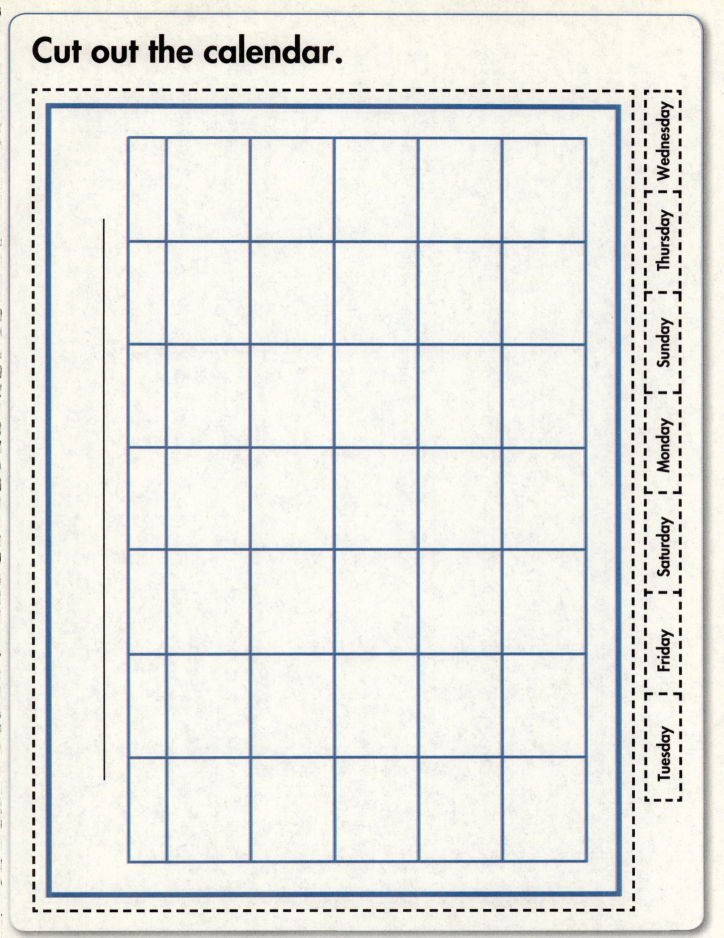

Draw times. Cut out the pictures.

Sunday

Monday

Tuesday

Wednesday

Thursday

Friday

Saturday

Cut out the cards.
Match the weather and clothes.

Cut out the cards. Act them out.

multiplying

dividing

adding

subtracting

singing

working on the computer

writing

measuring

kicking a ball

painting

reading

playing basketball

Cut. Make a meal. Write about it.

Cut. Draw and color.

paste

math

social studies

reading

science

Cut out the pages. Make a book.

What Are
They Doing?
by

Cut. Make a map. Show it to a friend.

Cut out the cards.

ball — 60 cents

apple — 17 cents

book — 1 dollar, 10 cents

pen — 3 cents

juice — 15 cents

banana — 45 cents

Cut. Act it out.